10/2/97

D0454664

For Nina —
who has helped
so many on their
journeys into the
light!

Love,
Luise

THE

HOUSES

ARE

COVERED

IN

SOUND

THE
HOUSES
ARE
COVERED
IN
SOUND

Louise Nayer

Bluelight Press

Grateful acknowledgement
is made to the editors of the
following magazines and anthologies in which
some of these poems were previously published:
"The Louisville Review,"
"Poetry Australia," "Poetpourri,"
and "The Southcoast Poetry Journal."

Special thanks to the California Arts
Council for awarding
Artist-in-Residence grants which
made the completion of
this project possible.

ISBN 0-9619744-2-7
Library of Congress Catalog Card Number
89-081826
Bluelight Press P.O. Box 642 Fairfield, Iowa 52556

Designed by Robin Terra

FOR

JIM

SARAH

AND

LAURA

TABLE OF CONTENTS

TRANSFORMATIONS

Lost and found,
found and lost.

Magic is twisting
absence into discovery.
          It is death.

We play in its skeletal maze
to find a warm rabbit
moving in a deep hole.

          It is birth,
              transformation,

                    what the earth
                    yields to the grass.

There was something
moving in a garbage can,
a white light
glowing in a spiral.
I thought it was a child,
no the wind, no the part
of myself that glowed.

I wanted to save
whatever was inside there
but was hungry
so walked into a corner store
and bought tiny donuts
wrapped in cellophane.
In the twilight
the cellophane shone.

Garbage in, garbage out,
I laughed to myself,
silencing my best thoughts
as if they would
take up arms against me.

In the Holland resistance,
"Give Terry a bone"
was a code word.
It let people in or out.
I heard an old man

with a war wound
tell it to a woman
who gave me towels
at the sauna.

I wanted to save
that phrase
because it had saved so many.

When I go to sleep now
certain words save me:
love, magic, stars, moon.

The glowing to the North,
the drinking gourd.

Something is always
giving off light.

They say, "It strengthens me."
They say it is an old man
who delivers the telegram with
stars on it. They say,
"My blood turned cold"
and "I couldn't move."
But they say the war
strengthens them; they find
they can survive anything, though
the ones that lost so much
have a strange emptiness
in their faces
and the Japanese woman
who carried a three week old baby
to a concentration camp in America
broke down and cried
and was embarrassed.
They say lipstick companies
turned to bullets;
women and children wandered
looking for work.
That in letters overseas
you had to read between the lines.
That babies were born to fathers who were
huddled in the fields of Normandy
clutching their guns
as their wives suckled
sons and daughters.

All they wanted
was to come home,
but coming home was filled
with nights of dreams.
"A time clock in his mind"
one wife said of her husband.
"He dreams of Normandy all the time."
And the new homes,
prefabricated, all the new things
coming off the production lines
that only months before had made
bombs, bullets, helmets, tanks and guns —
that nothing could make it
all right again.
America was a new country.
Everyone tried to be normal
so badly, it hurt
the corners of their mouths.
And the woman who cried
still felt embarrassed
because no one was crying anymore;
or if they did
they had to get up quickly to
kiss it and make it better.
And America became a
kiss it and make it better country.
The band-aids had stars and stripes,
and the kids wanted band-aids on everything,
even the slightest scratch.

The Christmas trees
are floating along the ocean,
a violent Pacific
dotted in green.

Death is like that,
something watery
and something else cut down
going across the foam
rapidly.

We were on a sailboat once.
You said it was like
turning in a circle.

For Ken

There is a bird
the size of an ocean
which moves
over the hushed dawn.

Its pink wings
glide across countries
and everyone
knows its name.

Paradise
rolls off the lips
of the dead.

They see
the sky flash orange
then green
before the sun drops.

Oh bird,
rising in a wave,
your songs say
ride, ride.

And on all the earth
the grasses grow tall,
tall enough to brush your feathers,

tall enough
to flutter
through your hollow bones.

My father wants to find
his father's grave
before he dies,
that first family
to return to,
to crawl inside
his mother's womb
and hear the voices
of his parents
whispering,
in the late night
of Paterson, New Jersey
after the drugstore closed.

My father said
he had sodas there.
They worked hard
and lost it
during the Depression.
He told me West Paterson
was fields then,
that he and his brother
were the only Jews
in the elementary school.

But I don't know
what he hasn't told me
or what I haven't listened to,
except the rise and fall

of his voice
or how his eyes tear
and all sounds drop
back into the earth.

I know his parents came from Vilna;
I saw it in a film once,
the center of Jewish culture,
artists and writers.

Half of me, my father's half,
wanders back there
to Lithuania, to the cold
northern winters
and tall books
to my grandmother's eyes.

She was overweight and died alone
on the Lower East Side.
I never met her
but in a picture I found
her eyes were the saddest eyes
I've ever seen.
I think my father took her eyes
into his soul.

But it's his father's grave
he looks for now,
the man who died when my father
was in the war in Persia,

the man who ran the drugstore
but was a poet, I'm told,
who wanted to read books at night,
who needed to read to survive.

I can't believe my father
doesn't know where his dead lie,
a series of erasures
that come back to haunt him
before he dies.

If souls must join
they need to know
where to go,
among which graves
to fly to, to weave
their dance of bones.

At night, my grandfather,
whom I never knew,
must call to his one living son,
to find the stone
under which he lies,
to rest a book upon that earth
and for someone, maybe me,
to write the story
of who lived and who died.

I remember holding on to words
spoken in cafes now closed to us.

The words live inside
my blue delft breakfast plate
        along the river Ijissle
        in the white chrysanthemums

        in the peculiar innocence
        of chaos.

In a little tin are my last cookies.

Next door, a boy is born
and lives in a drawer.

My paper supplies dwindle,
but I could give up words.

The sky is always ours
even though we are crowded together.

Someday, I will walk across the world.

For Anne Frank and Etty Hillesum

You sit among bougainvillea
painting pictures of the sea
on pods that my children
rattle in their magic rooms.

For 40 years
you have lived and died
in the sun and its shadows.

Every life is a miracle;
yours is a street of sand
that enters the sea.
Even in the black waters
there is the luminescence
of one who has been saved.

A small sea horse
floats into midnight.

For my sister, Anne, pregnant.

THE ACCIDENT

My blue fish
spawned a baby
in my dreams.
It was beautiful,
luminescent
among the quartz.

And how I longed
for perfection,
its gills
to be the opening
song of night.

One dead fish later
and your hands
aging, scarred,
on a white formica table

we all admit failure,
the accidents we could
not stop.

The ocean just across the street,
the older girl wailed
and still they burned.

The new renters
whisper about the
basement gas leak,
the doctor and his wife
rolling out flames
on the lawn.

And two young children
startled by screams.

The daughters imagine
what they can't see,
fireballs lighting the sky.

At night,
they try to stop the heat
that leaks in,
dream of two burned bathrobes
draped across a summer lawn.

They now believe:
those you love
disappear,
return broken.

Mornings,
they plunge into the sea
as the damaged skin
peels away
so much burning,
so much water.

For my parents burned
in an explosion, 1953

"The mountains lie back and melt
as one who has surfaced on the sun
and seen too much of nearly everything. "

Wendy Rose

She remembers mother's bandages.
Absence and burns.

The way her cheeks absorb sunlight
it is still gray
and she is not old.

When snow falls in the city
she dreams of lace and mountains.
Her skin is gorgeous
in the brisk air.

What is wrong is memory,
loss and disfigurement.
Her own face
becomes invisible at times
as if she is the burned one.

Long ago, her mother
entered the world
but the daughter became
the wound,
the scream,
the accident.

She sits behind windows
so very beautiful
looking at snow fall,
afraid to move,
as if to move
is to be hurt,
and to be hurt
is not to die,
but to live
and be wounded
so everyone can see.

It was summer,
time to bury the tears
in fresh earth.

We were pretending to heal
in a house full of mirrors
where mother's eyes
would rest
on her scarred, disfigured
face and hands
then turn away.

Father was out of the rocking chair
where he had moaned for one year,
sitting Shiva on a dead dream.

His scars receding,
he moaned only in his sleep now,
breathing mother's panic.

Mornings,
he took Anne and me
to Westhampton beach;
she read books beyond her age,
remembered words to please him,
lost the fat she'd gained.

This was the summer
we would all heal.

Anne and I monkeyed up trees,
muscled bodies tasty with sea salt,
everything growing
in the perfect ritual of summer,
our front yard orchard
of apple and pear trees.

I stayed by mother's side,
watched for disappearances,
jumped waves beyond the breakers,
turned red, brown, and freckled,
my blouses soft and light
patterned with butterflies and daisies.

We were healing slowly
though we knew mother's face
would never heal
even as Anne and I poured
over snapshots hidden away,
ivory and peach skin,
dark eyes like jewels.

She had been a natural beauty;
we wanted her face back.

It was summer.
The trees were filled with fruit
and for mother
this house too much
like the one that exploded,

the way salt wind
flooded the windows,
light white curtains,
bright sun and ocean nearby.

Waking from a restless sleep,
she ran to Anne's attic room,
brought her downstairs.

Father moved to the bannister,
face receding
into that old sadness.

Shaking me awake, she said,
"Something's about to happen.
I want us all together."

We sat around the long table.
Father held her hand;
we stared at each other,
the old terror revealed
in the middle of the night.

We were a new family.

Mother's face and hands
would never heal
and it was summer.
Everything was blooming.

At the shoe store
you chose patent leather.

"You can almost see your face in it."

When you returned from the fire,
you turned your face
away from your feet,
filled the closet with shoes,
buckles, bows,
wings of velvet,
anything
to fly away.

At night,
I looked out windows
imagining your bones
in the trees.
"Mama," I would sigh,
and the tree
was a blackened house.

Winter came and went
eight times
before the bandages came off.

When they did,
you had been wrapped up
forever.

II

I dreamt of miracles.
God opened the Red Sea;
Jesus healed lepers,
and the cripples of St. Saveur
walked from the cathedral door,
crutches hanging like crucifixes
from the high walls.

> "Woman burned in fire
>   saved by vitamin E."

You could read about it
in supermarkets.

The truth:
a famous surgeon
promised you the old face
guardedly.

Four Vietnamese girls
burned in the war
were chosen to come to the U.S.
for his treatment.

As he worked on you
one hot afternoon
he said, "You would never
have been chosen."

III

At the playground
I was Queen for a Day,
the leader of tragedy
gathering my tribe.

BURNED BAD BURNED BAD BURNED BAD

Then I ran through the housing project
harder and faster
than anyone my age.

I was running for my life.
A fire was chasing me.
It spread from flesh to trees
and even burned the ocean
in my dreams.

The shrieks of pain
settled among the grass and weeds.
Quietness set in like frostbite.
My eyes grew shy.

My skin broke in eczema,
red cracks, itching so bad
I too wanted to fly,
fly away from my body.

And when they stared at you
I pulled their eyes my way.

They tell me I'm pretty,
but sometimes
when my tongue
touches my lips
I can't find them.

Then I know
I'm looking
for the pieces of your face.

From the film *Pastoral Hide and Seek*

Birds and mother.
Always a flight.
        Terror mountain
        where wind and fog

                embrace a woman
                carrying a dead baby
                through the fields,

                the chill nestled
                in her arms.

In this illusion
a house exploded.

The frame
stands in the morning.

                Ashes sift through fingers.
                The charred smell is gone now

A child drowned,
covered in cold.

        Terror mountain
        where we go
        after our faces have cracked,

where we go to heal ourselves
where we go to die.

The blackbirds circling
and interminable night.

                    Come here.
                    Sit beside your childhood.
                    Drink from the old words.

You will grow strong
from this failed life.

                    You will find your own clock.
                    Listen, it's your heart.

Home

Lately I am in New Mexico,
watching an ocean
rise beyond a desert,
dreams to soothe
the dishes and laundry
that multiply like rabbits.

The children want
juice and scissors,
even the gum wrappers
that fall on the floor.

Between tasks, I scurry
into water,
dream I am a striped fish
floating near anemones.
When I float, I see everything.
When I float, my eyes
rise to the sky.

Sometimes even the children are slippery
and taking care they don't fall
is love. I hold them
wet and naked and it all comes back:
why we are here.

When I brush their hair,
the dreams go down their back,
glitter for a moment

as if their manes are sky
I paint stars on.

But the stars recede,
and I am propelled into a room
full of Cherrios and schedules,
propelled into the play
with its sudden conflicts,
its screams, its quiet tenderness.
Back in New Mexico,
the children are blue blossoms
in my hands.

They scent the whole sky
but do not say anything.

Quiet angels in their beds
take me there: to the millisecond
place of no tasks,
to the other women
whose bodies have filled
and emptied, whose houses
are covered in sound.

THREE FOR SARAH

Pouka, sweetpea, little one,
you have already doubled yourself.
With your china eyes and Egyptian head,
you are the oldest soul of all.

Rattling your way into night,
you are the perfect egg shape
dropped into afternoon,
an Indian dancer
twirling your puppeteer hands.

Oh hungry one,
waking with a scream in your throat,
I am the two breasts
walking in the night
to a hunger that can be satisfied.

I am the totem you seek:
sweet honey milk from a rain cloud,
sweet honey milk falling from a tree.

I I

My daughter drops words
on her plate,
                "horse, mine, eat."

Then she looks at her book
and whispers something
I do not know.

Outside and inside,
people are abandoning themselves
to the night.

But she is still talking,
more awake than the snow.

III

You turn on water faucets,
hear bumblebees
weaving a hive out your window.

"What is an accident? " you ask.
Oh, the things I could tell you.

"DaDa DaDa," sings your sister,
crawling like a snake
from room to room.
She picks up one thread
from your shredding blanket,
twirls it through her fingers.

I remember and remember and remember:
in a blue and white swimsuit
carried through the water,
in the constant voicing of my needs.

"Don't whine," my mother said
before me. And the gallon of milk
that broke against the linoleum
in the early morning.

It is a shock to be so young
with so many mistakes.

When I remember this,
I hug you against me.

She pulls a turtle
that squeaks across the floor
while a hawk
circles the evening sky.

They are preparing to eat,
talking of birds,
wounds and water.

The child reminds them
of themselves,
her body like the ones
they rolled down snowy fields in,
the fat little fingers
curled under mittens
against the penetrating
eastern chill.

They make room
for the past, present,
and future,
like swirling water
at twilight
when the last piece of sun
drops behind the world.

After dinner
she screams
like a river
smashing against a window
or being lost forever.

They gather her
in their arms,
light candles
through the house.

She looks at the flames,
listens to the murmurings
of those who hold her.

Then they all breathe together,
swallowing whatever
might keep them apart.

In my dreams,
cheap hotel rooms
explode in South America;

my two year old
is lost on beaches
and I search for her
in water, funky bars,
in my sister's arms.

When I wake:
my husband sleeps beside me
in a house that stands.

I put my hands on my belly
and hear my daughter's call,
"Mommy, get up."

Out the window,
a fluttering hummingbird
puts its beak into the feeder,
draws some nectar.

Sesame Street
replaces the nightmares.
Toast pops up
as my daughter watches
"Grouches Unite."

The dreams were about
mud patties,
small round circles

that fell apart in my hands.
I wanted to tell someone
but all around me
women were humming.

I don't know
what hasn't healed
inside of me.

Two years ago
a house was destroyed
while I was in labor.
I saw the hole
when I returned
with my new baby.

Now lights go on and off
in those rooms,
fireflies
across a dark hollow
of gardens.

The baby inside me was a tadpole;
it's now a big fish.
My daughter crawls backwards again,
says, "goo, goo"
into my tummy.

I dream of small children
meeting in a wooden house.
My belly is flat then
but the house is filled.

With a child just an eyedrop away,
I am the egg being timed,
the round belly of the moon,
the biggest house of all.

At midnight
the world is a wild heartbeat.

And in the earth,
the bones of the dead
tingle with the moon's light
as I walk by.
They dance in their bold boxes.

For I am new life,
the flower that survived the rains,
the moss in city concrete,
the clean green eye of the alley cat.

I am blood multiplying itself,
ten fingers dancing in water
and the wave on which you ride,
as you crest
between my legs,
with your necklace of foam,
with your necklace of blood.

ROUND MOON, BRIGHT LIGHT

For Laura Julia

I

Who are you
whom I failed to contact
for so long.
You were a wind in me
these months,
sea turning
the size of a thumb.

Forgive me
for not singing to you,
my small new fish,
the brother or sister
of my firstborn;

Who are you
living in the dark waters?
You are now a light
in my eyes; you are
helping me
return someplace
I cannot name,
oh small hands
small eyes, four month child.

II

The tiny spider
weaves its small web
on the bannister.
My daughter
is half asleep
but wakes
to the living creature.
"Baby bug," she chants,
"Baby bug."

She is wrapped in blankets,
out through two doors
to the back,
where jasmine
slinks over our neighbor's fence,
wild and aromatic.

The scented air will help her dream
like the lilac wands the women made
by the country swimming pool.
Witches and mothers
in a circle.

We sit on the grass now
and she settles down
until a dog barks.
"Dog, dog," she trumpets
with her head, her arms, her feet.

She carries all creatures in her soul.
She is a hawk, a fly, a cat, a minotaur.

Her head gets heavy
on my shoulder.
The dog has stopped barking.
The spider still weaves its web,
a tiny flash of life
hanging from the bannister.

In the quiet,
I can even hear the jasmine growing
if I listen deeply,
as deeply as Laura.

Sometimes we live in a bottle
with splitting seams,
with small TV's
and unsanitary toys
that get passed between children.

There is not enough soap in the world
to keep our bottle clean.

On a foolish day,
light with dreams,
we forgive everything
and float like contented fish.

We move between dust and crumbs
stirring and singing.
We love flawlessly.

On a weary day,
we are beached whales
dying on a dying shore
or small pekinese dogs
that snap at each other
and break the gifts
that were given to us:
blue stemmed glasses,
painted vases, music boxes,
sigh into the garbage
as we scream,
"More money, more money,

more money," like Paul
dying on his rocking horse.

What is it we rise to?
The momentary peace at night
when we sway in a gentle wind,
on an old canoe made
from the inside of a tree.

The ceiling's off now,
no walls.
We conjure twilight,
drink the stars.

We are luminescent now
as families can be
and wrap our children
in blankets
in the most ordinary gesture.

My daughter
brings her Barbie doll
into the bathtub
and dismembers her,
smears soap on the head
with its long blonde hair
and stirs her pretend coffee
with a right leg.

All over the city
three year olds
are collecting Barbies.

They plead for two or three,
even six or seven
with their glittery outfits
and long hair,
their sleek legs
and high heels.

Minutes later
I peek into the bathroom
to find she has wrapped the pieces
in a rainbow washcloth
which she delicately unfolds
then eats them
one by one:
leg, arm, head, torso and blue dress.
Satisfied,
she throws the parts
into the bathtub
then watches them float.

You teach me
how the red eye in the dark
pulses with blood,
and how the volcano
streams and bursts
with white light.

I pour your song
into glasses;
the red bird
and the purple feathers,
the pink blood
that announces you.

You are dancing
in a constant wind.
I have been gone
a thousand roads
from that place.

Now you bring me back
where old women dress me in satin,
let me sing
with lips of red wind.

With your crystal ball
and pink rose fingers,

you are the fortunate one,
travelling in a complete circle.

You teach me
the endlessness of string,
how we are all attached
like tiny red and white carnations
whose stems touch
at the bottom of a glass.

As music
fills the room,
the leaves float up
from the garden below.

Our fortunes
have come together,
marriage and children
among rocking chairs
and sunlight.

Downstairs, a woman
carries a child inside her.
We can hear her
near where the garden shimmers.

So much of my life
was about thought,
alone on the grass
or empty spinning.

I am surrounded
by touch now,
wild and constant.

We walk down the steep steps
to the garden below.

1000 copies printed at

West Coast Print Center

Berkeley, California

© *Louise Nayer 1990*